A Woman's Handy Booklet

Jyoti Kanda

MAPLE
PUBLISHERS

A Woman's Handy Booklet

Author: Jyoti Kanda

Copyright © 2024 Jyoti Kanda

The right of Jyoti Kanda to be identified as author of this work has been asserted by the author in accordance with section 77 and 78 of the Copyright, Designs and Patents Act 1988.

First Published in 2024

ISBN 978-1-83538-257-8 (Paperback)
     978-1-83538-258-5 (E-Book)

Book cover design and Book layout by:
    White Magic Studios
    www.whitemagicstudios.co.uk

Published by:
    Maple Publishers
    Fairbourne Drive, Atterbury,
    Milton Keynes,
    MK10 9RG, UK
    www.maplepublishers.com

A CIP catalogue record for this title is available from the British Library.

All rights reserved. No part of this book may be reproduced or translated in any form or by any means, electronic or mechanical, including photocopying, recording or by any information storage and retrieval system without written permission from the author.

This book is a memoir. It reflects the author's recollections of experiences over time. Some names and characteristics have been changed, some events have been compressed, and some dialogues have been recreated, and the Publisher hereby disclaims any responsibility for them.

Introduction

There is an importance of having self-time to implement goodness within ourselves Simple lists of examples for happiness are:

Allow time for yourself

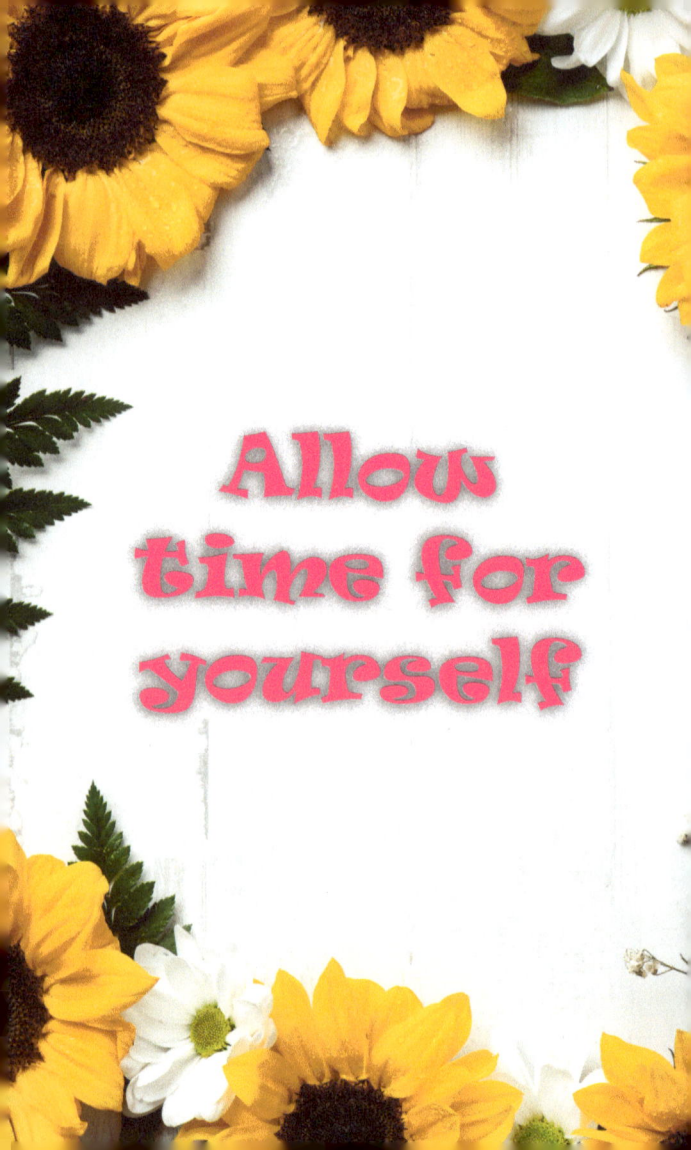

Realise the importance of oneself

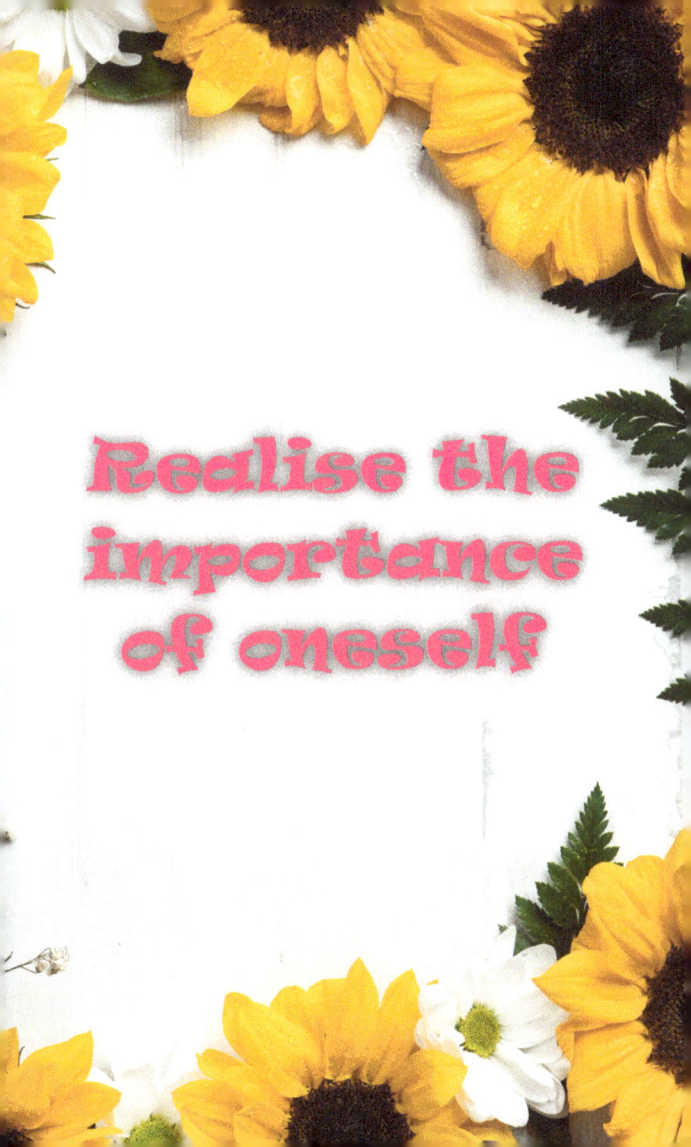

Strive for what you can

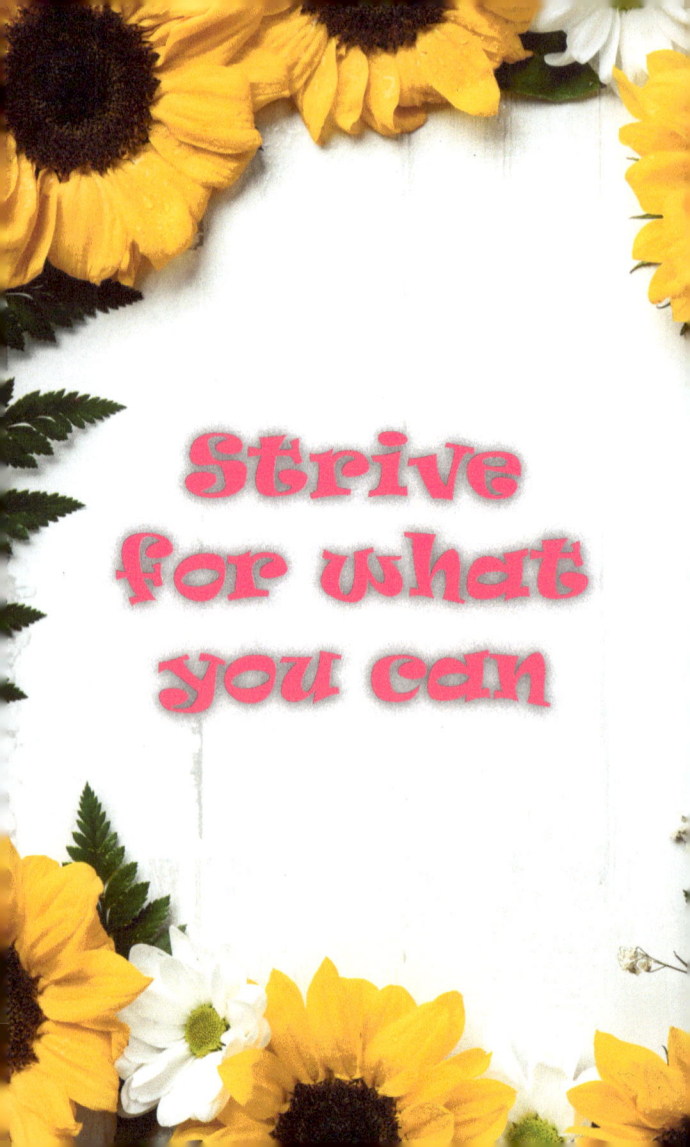

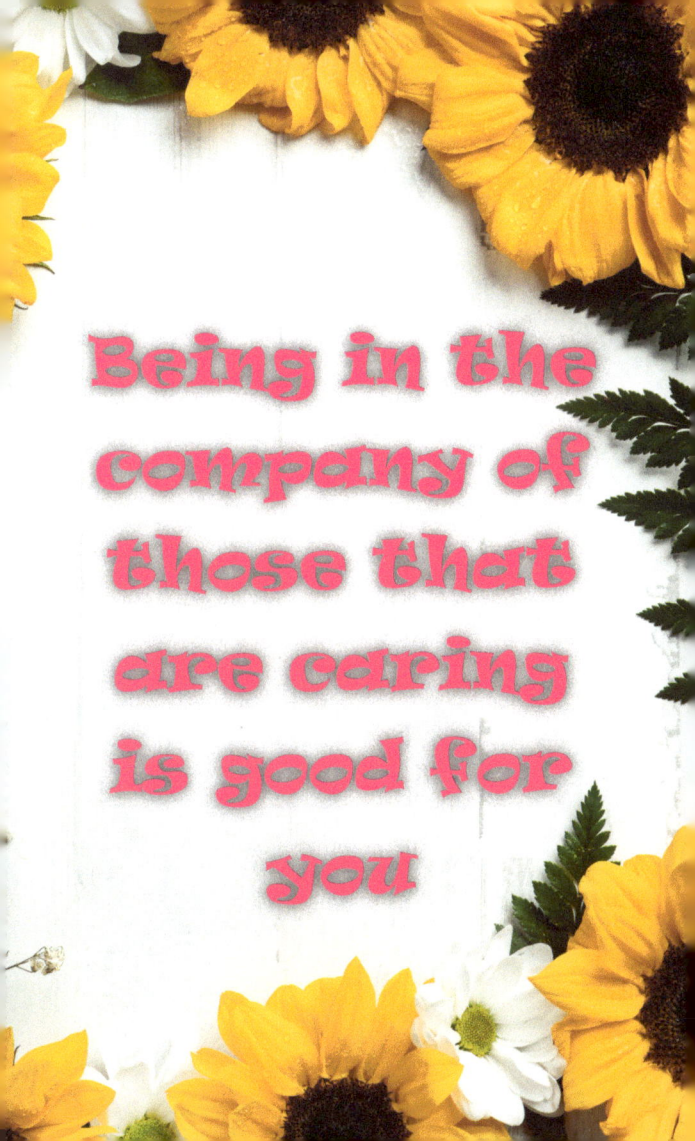
Being in the company of those that are caring is good for you

Always try to be positive

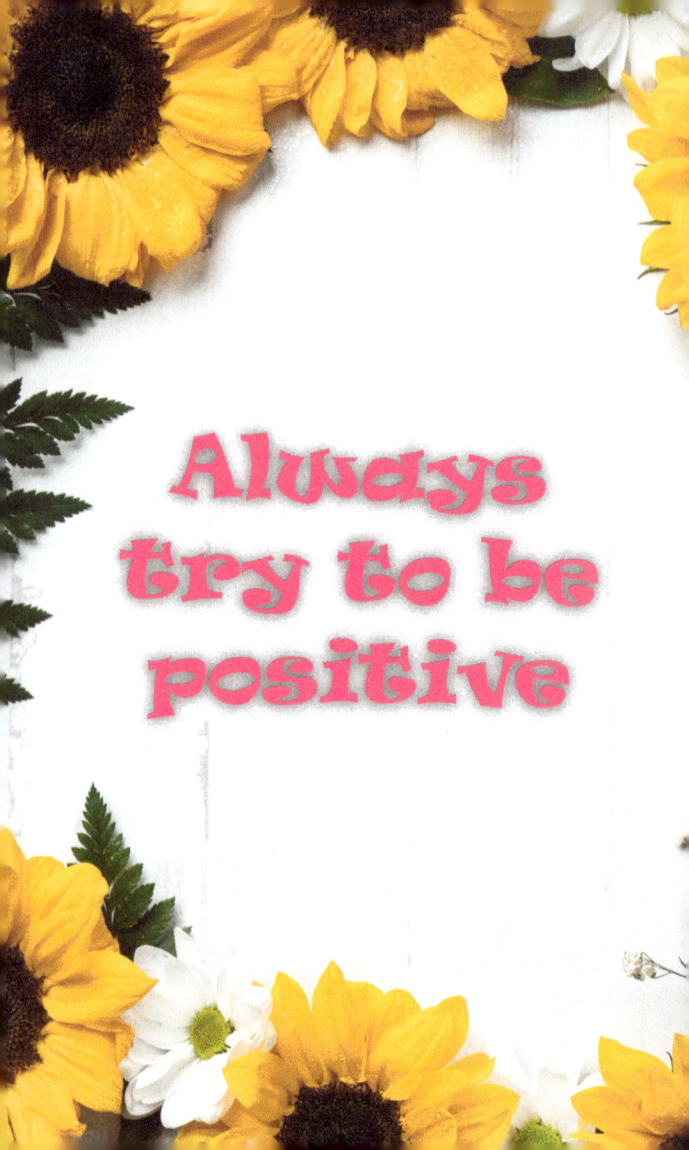

Live for the moment if you can

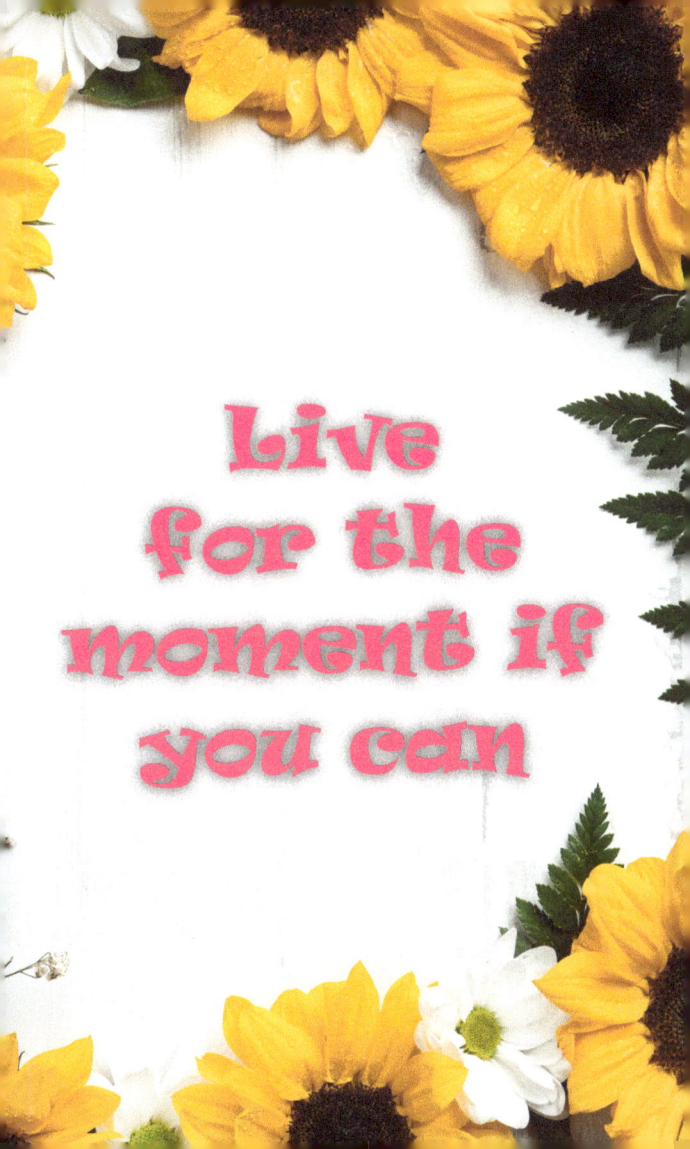

Don't let yourself down

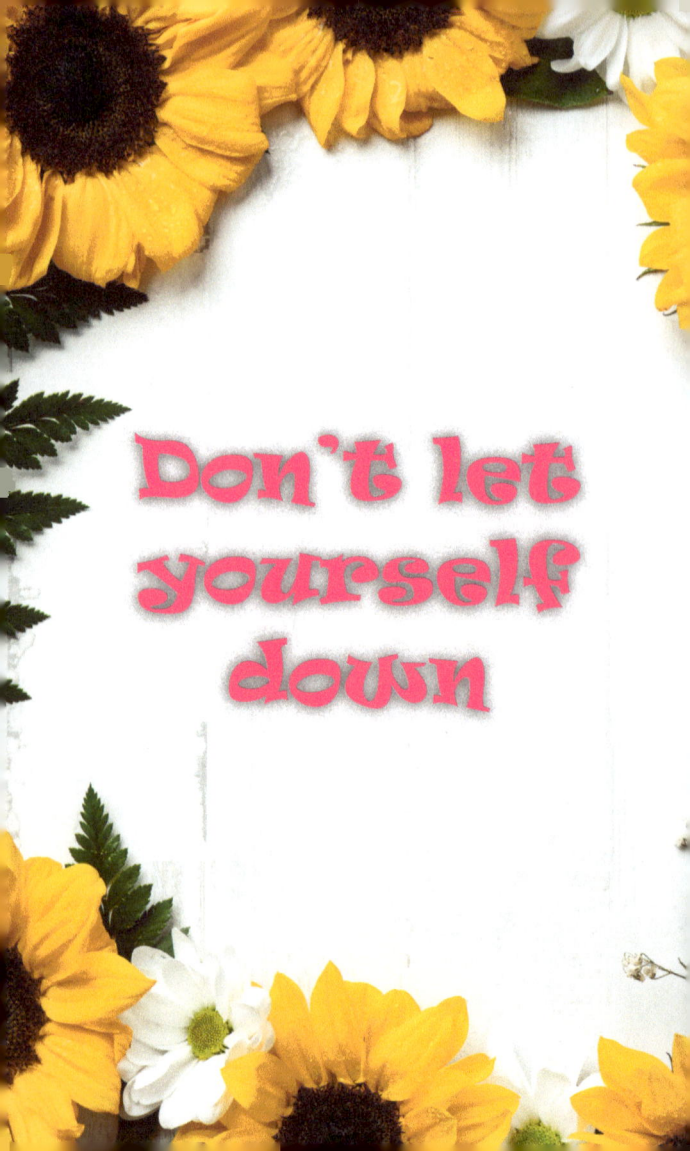

At the
end of
the day
just be
yourself

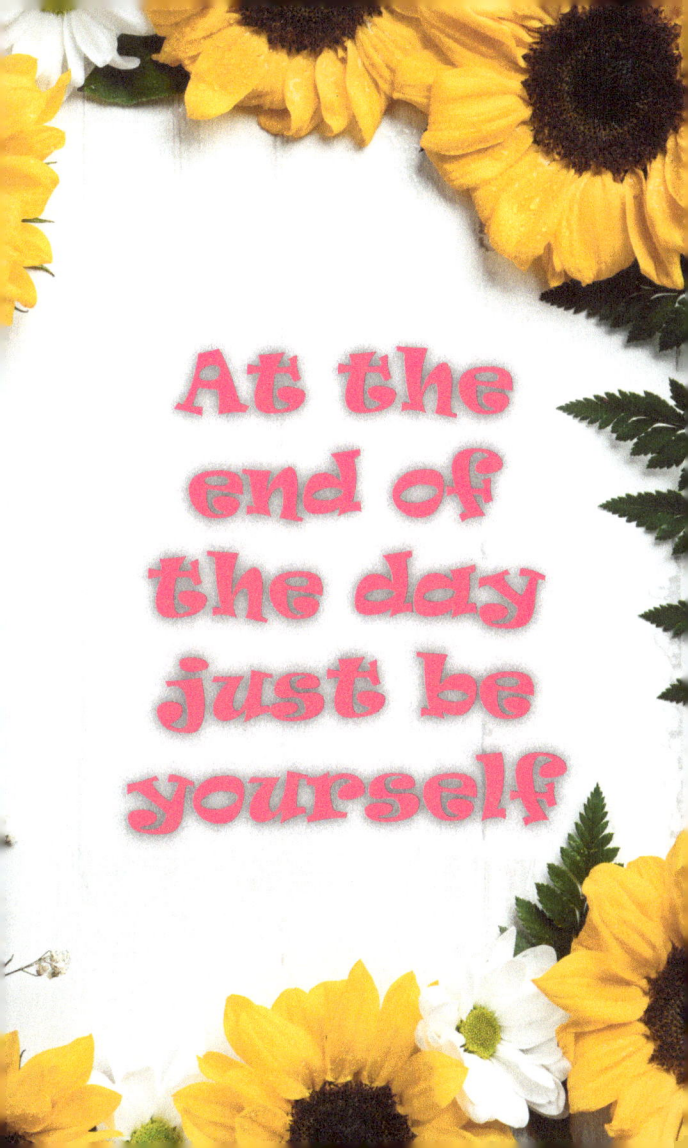

Even if somebody puts you down just keep going and be stronger

Always look forward to your next journey for positivity

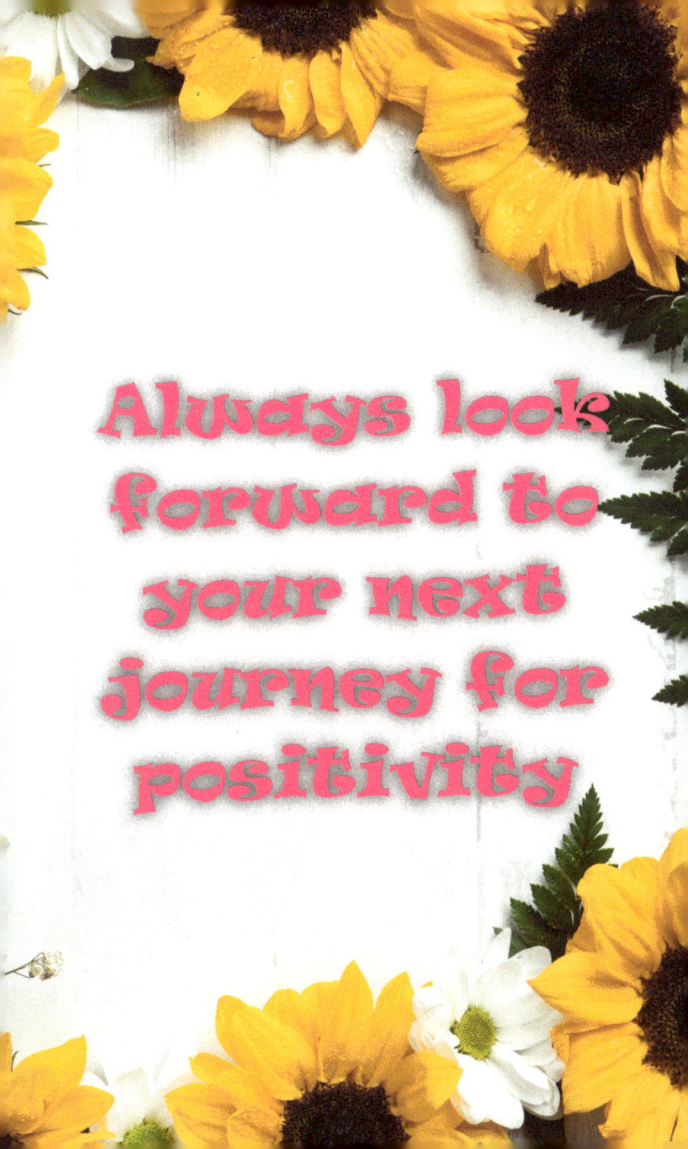

NOTES

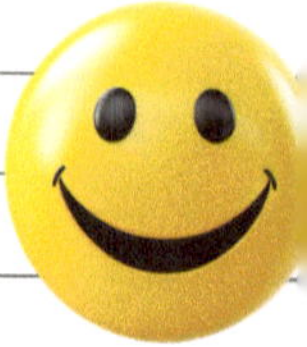

NOTES

NOTES

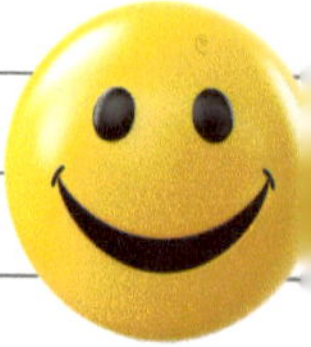

NOTES

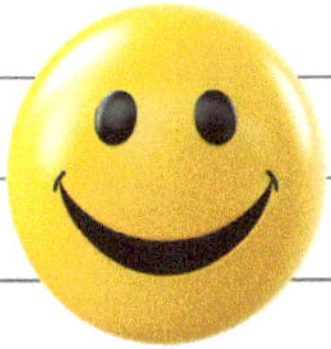

NOTES

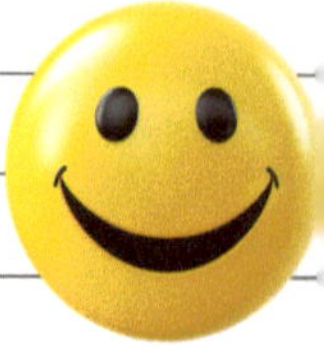

www.ingramcontent.com/pod-product-compliance
Lightning Source LLC
Chambersburg PA
CBHW040200100526
44590CB00001B/15